KODANSHA LIBRARY OF JAPANESE ART

No. 6

Plate 2. PUPPY. *Hanging scroll, ink painting. Yasuda Collection.*

俵 屋 宗 達

TAWARAYA SOTATSU

(active early 17th century)

Edited by
ICHIMATSU TANAKA

English text by
ELISE GRILLI

CHARLES E. TUTTLE COMPANY
Rutland, Vermont — Tokyo, Japan

NOTE ON THE ENGLISH TEXT

For the Japanese-language edition of this book Professor Ichimatsu Tanaka provided an excellent text with a summation of the recent work of Japanese scholars on Sotatsu (see Bibliography on page 86). Though the present book contains the same selection and arrangement of plates as originally made by Professor Tanaka, with his approval I have written an entirely new text and captions from the viewpoint of the Western reader rather than the Japanese reader he was addressing. I have tried to separate Sotatsu from the other men with whom his work has been confused and also to indicate his importance in the formation of a specifically Japanese decorative style. More could not be attempted in the modest confines of this small volume.

E. G.

Published by the Charles E. Tuttle Company, of Rutland, Vermont & Tokyo, Japan, by arrangement with Kodansha, Tokyo. All rights reserved by Kodansha, without whose written permission no part of the contents of this book may be reproduced.

First English edition. May. 1956

Third printing, 1960

Library of Congress Catalog Card No. 56-8491

Printed in Japan
by Toppan Printing Co., Tokyo

SOTATSU

If only five names were to be chosen from the entire history of Japanese art, one among them would indubitably be that of Tawaraya Sotatsu—and there are those who would place him even among the first three greatest artists of his land. This admiration and high evaluation has come about rather suddenly and is a very recent phenomenon, a product of the past thirty years. Every epoch looks at the past through its own lenses, and apparently there is some quality in the style of Sotatsu which appeals intimately to modern eyes, a strength of "abstract design" which brings him close to present-day international desiderata of decorative emphasis above representational content. In addition, Sotatsu played an important role in the formation of an original, decorative, and specifically Japanese art during the Momoyama period (1573–1615), after a long subservience by Japanese artists to the influence that flowed from T'ang and Sung China. In his own day, in the Kyoto of the early seventeenth century, Sotatsu also enjoyed a position among the artists in court circles and, what is even more significant, stood in the immediate entourage of Hon-ami Koetsu, the "Leonardo da Vinci of Japan," the versatile genius in whom all the arts and refinements of his day seemed to find their confluence.

With such eminence, then and now, it is hard to believe that the very name of Sotatsu could have almost disappeared for over two hundred years, during which his fame ebbed away entirely and his works lost their identity among attributions to far lesser men upon whom history, for some reason, bestowed her fickle smile. Thus it became a task of almost archeological nature to excavate his work from the obscuring dust—and the task is not yet finished. There still remain a goodly number of problems which obscure the personality of the artist and provoke scholars to endless disputes regarding the authenticity of various works assigned to Sotatsu and his school. Despite all these doubts and questions, however, there yet stands forth in a clear light the figure of a very great artist, of a painter of such creative power that (to paraphrase Voltaire) did we not know him we should have to invent him. But the case is not quite so drastic. Our present age and our instruments of appreciation have already gathered power for such resuscitation through experience in similar tasks. Not long ago the name and works of El Greco were equally obscured by time; that artist, as we know him today, was brought back from the dead in the first decade of our century, after the vision of Cezanne and the German expressionists had freshly sharpened our appreciation for his strange talents.

Still closer, perhaps, is the parallel with the decline and rise of the fame of Shakespeare—and for reasons not far different. Like Shakespeare, Sotatsu was a non-academic artist, a man whose gifts propelled him forward by a route other than the accepted one of schools and apprenticeships, of orthodox training along well-worn paths. Shakespeare's formal schooling amounted to "a little Latin and less Greek"; yet, lacking the university training expected of the poets and dramatists of his day, he had nevertheless built up an amazing corpus of classical scholarship and of understanding of the phenomena of nature. In a similar manner, Sotatsu's training in art did not proceed obediently along the paths laid out by the academies of the Kanos or the Tosas of his day, although he came to know their methods and their secrets, either by some minimum of schooling (legend does make him the pupil of a Kano, either Eitoku or Sanraku) or, what is far more likely, by a process of auto-didactic imbibing. For a craftsman's son, living in the art-impregnated atmosphere of Kyoto and befriended by Koetsu, this was not too impossible a feat.

Academicians, however, are generally suspicious of such irregularly trained geniuses, and orthodox art historians are equally baffled by, if not actually hostile to, such strange upstarts. Neither Shakespeare nor Sotatsu was surrounded by the type of men who take notes and keep records, who annotate and transmit detailed biographical information. Documentary sources in both cases are so scant that they conjure up only a shadow of a personality and give rise to

6

more problems than can be answered by the usual tools of scholarship. Final decisions as to attribution and interpretation must come from the internal evidence of the works themselves.

The social conditions that cradled Sotatsu also showed some points of affinity with those of Elizabethan England. In both cases there was a moment of free flux in social stratification, which made it possible for unusual men to rise through their native gifts. There was a shift in feudal alignments and the beginning of an emerging bourgeoisie. There was an influx of new ideas—in England through geographical exploration and the new learning, and in Japan through the continental campaigns of Hideyoshi and his receptivity to the arts and sciences imported by the Portuguese, Spanish, and Dutch. Even the withdrawn and world-remote aristocracy of Kyoto felt the new current, but only for a brief moment, before the Tokugawa shoguns slammed shut the door to the outer world. Fifty years earlier or fifty years later the times would not have been encouraging to the unfolding of Sotatsu's genius.

One final point of affinity between the fates of Shakespeare and Sotatsu deserves mention. Both men rose from lowly stock and were fortunate in reaching an aristocratic audience that provided them the satisfaction of a fully aesthetic appreciation of their art, beyond the popular acclaim of a wider public. Both hobnobbed for a short time with the highest court circles, where they were valued in their own time for the evident gifts they brought to this world of refined and leisurely consumption. That these similarities of fate should have occurred almost at the same point of time at opposite ends of the world can be dismissed as coincidence or it can open an avenue for historic and social speculation. The resemblance is here adduced primarily to help clarify, for Western readers, a set of circumstances and a personality that can be better understood through such parallels. The comparison with Shakespeare is not intended to elevate the stature of Sotatsu, but to insist that, before either artist became sanctified by later enthusiasts, he was a struggling and practical craftsman, working with his hands and with his creative ingenuity in a workshop atmosphere of commissions, revisions, assistants, and imitators. Therein reside the roots of the many pieces of patchwork and the incongruities that confuse the logical analyst.

Neither Sotatsu's birthplace nor the year of his death can be fixed with any degree of assurance. We know that he was active in the year 1602, when he is reported to have aided Koetsu in repairing the famous sutra scrolls which the Taira family had donated to the Itsukushima Shrine in 1164. The fact that Sotatsu was entrusted with work on so precious a relic indicates that he had already established himself as a painter of proven ability.

We know further that by the year 1630 Sotatsu had earned the rank of *hokkyo,* bestowed only on artists of maturity and high achievement. This fact is substantiated by the most important single document relating to Sotatsu, namely the inscription by the hand of the courtier and poet Karasumaru Mitsuhiro, found as a colophon at the end of the pictorial scroll of the *Life of Priest Saigyo* (*Plate 48*). This inscription reveals far more than the fact that Sotatsu was living and at the height of his activity in the year 1630. It proves also—as the painting indeed substantiates—that Sotatsu had a special understanding of the ancient Japanese art of Yamato scroll painting, so that he was called in to make a copy of a scroll which Mitsuhiro borrowed from the imperial archives for the purpose.

There exists also a mention of Sotatsu in a letter written by Sen Shoan, a son of the famous tea-master Sen Rikyu. Here the writer states that he was invited to a tea ceremony by Tawaraya Sotatsu, indicating thereby that Sotatsu was part of that circle of Kyoto tea-masters and aesthetes who were so influential in establishing a new trend in the arts. Since Shoan died in 1614, this letter must antedate that year.

A remaining letter, from Sotatsu's own hand, is not dated, but it is important in associating him with the Daigoji in Kyoto. This letter is really a brief note, addressed to Priest Kaian of that temple, thanking him for a gift of some boiled bamboo shoots. The Daigoji still owns two important works by Sotatsu, the screen of the "Court Dance" (*Plates 42 & 43*) and a fan screen (*Plates 21 & 22*), and from the Daigoji also stems the screen of the *Tales of Genji* (*Plates 6 & 7*), now in the Seikado Foundation, Tokyo. The signature on the letter is, of course, of the greatest importance.

One or two other scraps of brief mention are found in letters and in diaries of the time. These bits of information are more confusing than illuminating. We are not sure whether the same person is in question. We cannot even determine with certainty whether Sotatsu was the son of a textile merchant or of a fan-maker in Kyoto. His name is also found in a family genealogical record that would make him related to Koetsu by marriage, since the two men are said to have wedded two sisters. And that completes the pitifully scant data regarding a man who is now considered to have been one of the great creative figures in Japanese art.

The histories of art can only state that Sotatsu was "active in the first part of the seventeenth century." The relationship with Koetsu would indicate that they were fairly close in age and that Sotatsu's life span may have fallen roughly between the years 1570 and 1640.

Far more eloquent than these biographical fragments is the language of the paintings that Sotatsu created. Of these only a bare handful are now definitely assigned to him and said to be *by* Sotatsu, while many more are *attributed* to him or to his followers. Several works carry a signature "Sotatsu" and a circular seal "Inen." This last word has no clear meaning and is taken to be a fanciful name for his school or atelier. The occurrence or absence of this signature and seal has become the cause of endless disputes among scholars. In the present brief discussion, however, it will be wiser to avoid this labyrinth and consider the far less provocative evidence contained within the works themselves.

At the very center of all stylistic analysis stands the Saigyo scroll (*Plate 48*), the one work with a trustworthy inscription, not by the artist himself, but by Karasumaru Mitsuhiro, whose style of writing is too well known to be easily imitated. Of course we are here dealing not with an independent creation,

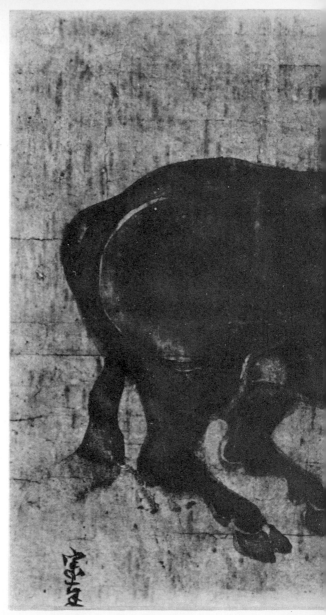

Plate 3. BULLOCK.
Hanging scroll, ink
painting. Chomyoji,
Kyoto.

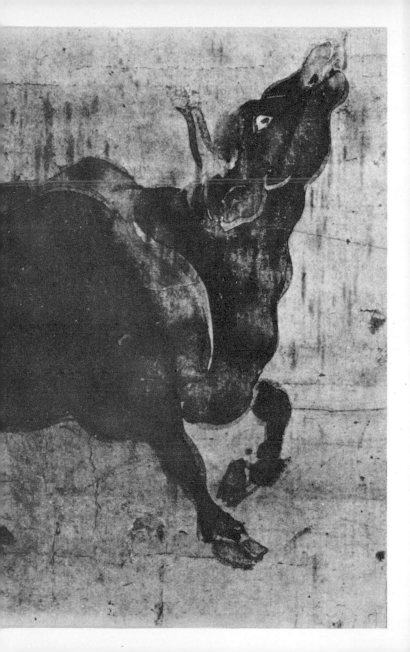

but with the attempt by an artist to recapture the contents and the flavor of a painting several hundred years old. This is, then, a retelling of an ancient tale, but we may well assume that there was no need to disguise the quality of the individual's "handwriting" in the new version. That was not expected of Sotatsu. What his clients desired was a copy of the contents, of the pictorial narration, with some adherence to the style of the original. The degree of closeness to his model is actually Sotatsu's own desire and goes "beyond the call of duty." It arises from his own interest in the style of Yamato painting, the characteristic Japanese manner of painting of some three or four hundred years before Sotatsu's day, an archaistic interest that is confirmed by many other instances scattered throughout his works.

A close study of the Saigyo scroll reveals many elements that we have come to associate with Sotatsu's style. He followed the design conventions of figures and perspective that are found in the scrolls of the Kamakura period, but the line quality is the typically soft "Sotatsu line." The coloring of the original version followed the high key and clear tones of Yamato pictures, while Sotatsu added those characteristic, wet over-paintings of darker and richer color blots which are called *tarashikomi* in Japanese. (The clearest examples of this technique in our series of plates may be seen in the detail of the pine in *Plate 16,* the paddy field in *Plate 23,* and the background of the flying thunder god in *Plate 26*). The result is a rounding of forms and an enrichment of surface. Sometimes Sotatsu is credited with the invention of this technique, but it is far more likely that this is a development in color of the wet "splash ink" method known to Sesshu and many other painters in Japan and in Yüan China.

From the pines and rocks of the Saigyo scroll a clear bridge leads via the paintings on the Yogen-in doors (*Plates 36–38*) to a similar broad simplification and patterning found on the great screen of "Pine Islands" in the Freer Collection, Washington. Thus Sotatsu added his own touches to the archaistic work he was asked to perform in copying the old scrolls and, at the same time, derived a great understanding of technique and narrative procedure in the ancient Japanese manner. How intimate his knowledge of the Yamato paintings must have been we can surmise from the echoes found in his work of many specific details derived from such scrolls as the *Tales of Heike, Long-Nosed Goblins, Shigisan Engi, Fast Bullocks, Tales of Genji*, and many others.

This turning back to a previous epoch in Japan's own art history is a significant symptom of the Momoyama style, which later developed into the Kyoto painting of the next two centuries. It should be recalled that there were internal and external historic reasons for this retrospective interest in Japan's own art achievement. Japan had received a second great wave of Chinese cultural dominance, together with the influx of Zen Buddhism, which set in around the year 1200. By the middle of the sixteenth century this wave had spent itself. Korea, the usual geographic transmitter between China and Japan, had become the declared enemy during Hideyoshi's campaign in 1594. After the death of this general, the first Tokugawa shogun, Ieyasu, confirmed Japan's policy of gradual withdrawal from foreign contacts. China under the last Ming emperors had far less to offer Japan than she had done in the days of her greatest glory under the T'ang and Sung dynasties. And Japan, at the same time, was beginning to feel herself a country of cultural maturity and of economic stability, all of which was conducive to greater self-confidence and national pride. The idealistic and philosophically muted Chinese ink-paintings that had so delighted the Ashikaga shoguns were out of key with the craving for resplendent wall decorations of the Momoyama generals or the Tokugawa shoguns. Even Kyoto, which looked down its aristocratic nose at the efforts of the nouveau riche upstarts in Nagoya, Osaka, and Edo—even Kyoto was growing away from Chinese subtleties and developing a new Japanese elegance of its own. The ingredients of this new art movement were partly the elements derived from a revival of the art of the Late Heian period (897–1185), an epoch when Japan had been almost self sufficient in her cultural development; partly, also, Kyoto was fortunate in developing a circle of original artists, who relished the revival of ancient forms, but who developed their own vision and their own aesthetics.

Out of traditional materials and out of deliberately archaistic subject matter, Koetsu, Sotatsu, and their followers created a sort of Japanese Renaissance in which the refinements of the Heian period were transmuted into a more monumental decorative style. They retained the intuitively "felt" placement, the perspective, the conventional stylizations of water and foliage, and the bright colors of Yamato painting, but enlarged the vision from illustrated scrolls to large screens of many panels, intended to be seen across vast spaces, indoors or outdoors. Sotatsu's special contribution, unequalled by his contemporaries or his followers, with the possible exception of Korin, was a dynamic composition that transcended purely decorative space arrangements.

The encompassing circle, the equator of this art world in Kyoto was the tea cult, the "way of tea," which may start from a cup of green tea enjoyed by a few congenial friends in a humble hut, but leads outward into a whole world of thought and morality, of man's relation to universal harmony. The two poles around whom this idea revolved were Sen Rikyu, its ideological interpreter, and Hon-ami Koetsu, who expressed a transcendent idea through natural materials, through pottery, through painting, through poetic writing. From the teaching and the practice of these two men there developed an art that summed up Japanese aspirations of past centuries and indicated a new direction which has not seen its end even today.

Koetsu was able to translate into tangible materials and new designs the deep-rooted Japanese conviction that nature is a divinity and that man can create only as nature creates. The raw materials of clay and sand, of wood and stone, of metals and ores, of water and rosin, of pulpy fibers and the silky web of a moth, all this he knew as an artist knows, through every vein and nerve of his body. He had a poetic or intuitive or "natural" way of handling and arranging these materials and he had also the poet's or the prophet's ability to inspire others with his fervor. Artists and craftsmen congregated around him. In 1615 Tokugawa Ieyasu gave him a grant to a stretch of land in Takagamine, on the north-western edge of Kyoto. There Koetsu built a villa and gathered around himself craftsmen in all media, until the settlement could rightly be called an "artists' village."

Just what part Sotatsu played in this circle around Koetsu is difficult to determine, but there are ample traces of a rather close collaboration. There exist a number of scrolls with poems written in Koetsu's fine hand, one of the greatest achievements in Japanese calligraphy. The writing is placed on paper that is decorated with flowers, trees, vines, or deer, all lightly painted in pale washes of gold or silver dust (see *Plate 40*). These decorations form a subtle counterpoint to the poetry and move as a sort of frieze, appearing and disappearing. In no way do they try to illustrate the poems directly, but provide a muted undercurrent that echoes the mood and rhythm of the poems. These paintings were once believed to stem from Koetsu himself, but are now generally recognized as Sotatsu's contribution to a very sentitive and intimate form of collaboration. The painter's work came first, apparently under the close supervision of Koetsu, and entirely in a spirit of harmony with the poetic script, which was added later.

If Sotatsu really was a brother-in-law of Koetsu's as the genealogical legends would have it, it was certainly more than nepotism that led Koetsu to assign this work to his relative. More likely it was the other way around—that Koetsu recognized special talent in a young craftsman. The young man did not have full academic training as a painter? All the better, then, for he was not hardened in any Kano or Tosa tradition. Koetsu readily recognized some special ability, and he gave the young man work of more and more responsibility. First he allowed him to repair the Taira sutras, under his own direct supervision; then came the work of copying various ancient scrolls; then, perhaps, there developed that joint work on the poetic scrolls. By that time the young man must have been a frequent visitor in Koetsu's home, thus coming to know and to marry the younger sister of

Plate 4. WATER FOWL IN A LOTUS POND.
Hanging scroll, ink painting. Hara Collection.

Plate 5. WATER FOWL IN A LOTUS POND.
Hanging scroll, ink painting. Magoshi Collection.

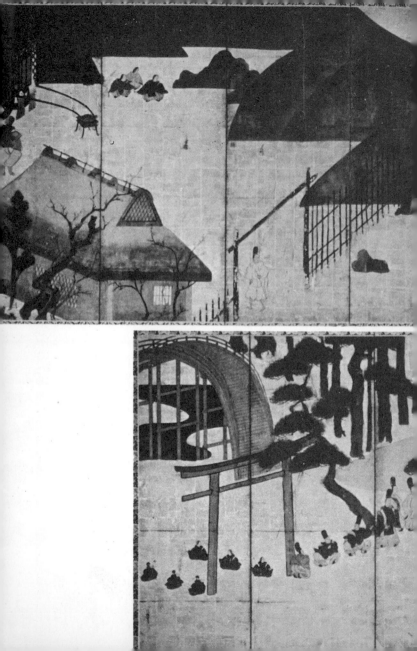

Plates 6 & 7. TALES OF GENJI. *Pair of six-panel screens ("Sekiya" at top, "Miotsukushi" at bottom), color and gold foil on paper, 157 ×263 cm. each. Seikado Foundation, Tokyo. See Plates 11–16 for details.*

Koetsu's wife. And all this time the younger man unfolded a natural talent, which Koetsu guided to the point where Sotatsu could spread his wings and embark on the original work of the *Tale of Genji* screens (*Plates 6 & 7*), to be followed by still more untrammeled creations in the screens of the "Court Dance" (*Plates 42 & 43*) and the "Gods of Wind and Thunder" (*Plates 17–20*).

There is no documentary evidence to substantiate this imaginary development—but neither is this an idle fancy that is not borne out by the clues within the works. There is a rising maturity from one work to another in a series of Sotatsu's works, just as the plays of Shakespeare grow in stature from the earlier comedies to the later tragedies. And again Sotatsu offers a parallel in the lessening dependence on historical chronicles and older styles or mannerisms. The final works in each case are achievements so original and so strange in their own time that they had to await full appreciation several centuries after their creation.

Sotatsu cannot be said to have founded a school, with apprentices and close followers in the Japanese manner. Sosetsu, who is said to have been Sotatsu's son, is but a weak echo of the master. Korin (1658–1716), born almost

one hundred years after Sotatsu, did, however, grasp to the full the implications of archaic Japanese subject matter coupled with a new force of decorative design. Korin learned from Sotatsu in the typical Oriental way of reverential copying, which still survives in Korin's precise renditions of the "Gods of Wind and Thunder" (Tokyo Museum) and the "Matsushima" screen (Boston Museum). Around Korin there gathered a group of artists who are generally called *Rimpa* (Korin School), and these men formed a living link with Sakai Hoitsu (1761–1828). Even today the artists of *Nihonga* (traditional Japanese painting) recall nostalgically the themes and the style of Sotatsu.

In addition to his big works in color, Sotatsu left a number of paintings in *sumi* ink only (*Plates 2–5, 39, 41*). *These* smaller paintings are "minor works" only as to size. In their intrinsic artistry they stand beside the monumental screens—if I may resort to a final comparison with the English bard—much as the sonnets stand in relation to the great tragedies. There is no known scale to measure such proportions.

Plate 10

COURT DANCE SCREENS : DETAIL

See Plates 42 & 43 for entire screens.

The two screens from which this detail comes (*Plates 42 & 43*) form one compositional unit, even though each screen can stand as a separate composition, and each panel, in fact, has its own vital existence. Like the dance itself, the movement of the design originates at the lower right and moves diagonally across to the extreme left ; there it terminates in a circular group that directs the eye back to the central four dancers. Such controlled movement in an endlessly dynamic composition bespeaks an artist of a high order, with a rhythmic sense as strongly developed as that of Rubens, who, strangely enough, was Sotatsu's exact contemporary. Of course, the comparison must not be pushed too far, for in place of the Fleming's impetuous vivacity and luxurious avalanche of rich detail, the Japanese artist eliminates, deliberates, symbolizes, and moves with dignified restraint— again like the character of the ancient court dance that forms his theme.

The immediate inspiration for these screens might have come to the painter from the version of this scene found in the Kamakura period picture scrolls, which he must have known very well, or—and this seems the far more likely and least roundabout explanation—from actual performances at court, which he likely had opportunity to witness in Kyoto.

Sotatsu seized upon the brilliant colors of the costumes and the drums and placed these rich rainbow hues against a golden ground, thus to create one of his most glowing designs. No other work from his hand achieves this almost barbaric splendor of a maharajah's huge rubies and emeralds in a lavish golden setting. It should be recalled that this ancient *bugaku* entertainment of the court came to Japan from Korea, perhaps in the eighth century, and that its real roots go back far beyond that date, probably to India.

The golden background, with its suggestion of unspecified space, allows Sotatsu to omit the realistic localization of the platform that serves as the usual stage for this dance. The

(*continued on page 78*)

Plates 11 & 12 (following)

"Tales of Genji" Screens : Details from "Sekiya"

See Plate 6 for entire screen. Shown here are the gate-keeper's house and Utsusemi's carriage (Plate 11) and Genji's carriage (Plate 12).

Sotatsu repeatedly drew on *Tales of Genji* for themes. This pair of large screens (shown in entirety in *Plates 6 & 7* and in detail in the following six plates), based on the "Sekiya" and "Miotsukushi" scenes of the famous novel, stands close to the center of the Sotatsu attributions; their internal and external evidence, though perhaps not absolutely conclusive in a court of law, is yet convincing enough to let this work serve as a criterion of Sotatsu's style.

The two screens are unified in narrative, since they both represent incidents of Genji's meeting with a former love, but compositionally they are quite separate. In this respect they differ from the screens of the "Ivy Lane," "Court Dance," and "Wind and Thunder Gods," where each pair is held together by inner tensions of design. The Genji screens are less emphatically decorative and still rather close to their source in the Yamato picture scrolls, indicating perhaps an earlier stage of the artist's development from illustration to independent composition.

The screen called "Miotsukushi" (*Plate 7*) represents the meeting of Prince Genji with his former love, Akashi-Himegimi, in front of the Shinto shrine Sumiyoshi, at the seashore. The panels are crowded with small figures and with landscape details which all derive quite faithfully from

(*continued on page 28*)

Plate 12

Plate 13

" Tales of Genji " Screens :   Detail from " Miotsukushi "

See Plate 7 for entire screen.

(continued from page 24)
the Japanese tradition of narrative scroll paintings.   The figure types, the method of stylization of pines and waves, the large cart, and the rearing bullock at the lower right can all be traced to parallels in the old scrolls with which Sotatsu was familiar.   These are echoes from the arts, literary and pictorial, of the Heian period, some four hundred years back, to which the aesthetes of Kyoto felt particularly drawn. The artistic circle around the famous Koetsu, of which Sotatsu also formed a part, enacted a veritable renaissance of the elegance and refinement of the Fujiwaras that is so eloquently described in the pages of *Genji*.

However, this ancient vocabulary of narrative and painterly conventions was freely rearranged by Sotatsu to erect monumental and decorative designs that were new and personal creations ; herein we see a contrast to the Tosa school, which continued to repeat the old formulae until they became ever more tenuous and feeble.   The new breath that Sotatsu infused can be felt in the big diagonal curve of the shore line, with bold counter-curves of people and trees coming up from bottom left.   New also is the almost " abstract " play of verticals and curves in the bridge at upper left.   In addition to these beginnings of a new decorative force, there
(continued on page 30)

Plate 14

"TALES OF GENJI" SCREENS: DETAIL FROM "MIOTSUKUSHI"

See Plate 7 for entire screen. Shown here is the boat in which waits Genji's former ladylove.

(continued from page 28)
is a psychological innovation in the hidden emotional drama of the invisible heroines who remain secreted in boat and carriage, respectively, on each screen.

Decorative and psychological strength are developed still further in the second screen, called "Sekiya" (*Plate 6*), where Prince Genji is shown at the encounter with Utsusemi at the barrier station Aisaka. Here Sotatsu has selected his design elements and placed them almost like a good stage director, intent on extracting the greatest dramatic force from a given situation. The setting is reduced to the barest elements of mountain, gate, and gate-keeper's house, each placed at a sharp angle, so that there results an exciting series of dynamic oppositions and rapid zig-zag alternations, portending an emotional conflict in the offing. Genji, whose carriage seems to have just arrived from a place around the jutting mountain ridge, is barely indicated by the red accent of sleeve projecting from carriage (*Plate 12.*) The bullock is still straining forward in his motion and starts the eye of the observer on the invisible path that leads to Utsusemi's brother, who is about to receive the letter, which he is then to carry past the gate-keeper, into the inner enclosure, and on to the carriage where his sister is waiting in suspense.

(continued on page 32)

Plates 15 & 16

"TALES OF GENJI" SCREENS: DETAILS FROM "MIOTSUKUSHI"

See Plate 7 for entire screen.

(continued from page 30)
The active drama is centered in the group of arrival at the right, but equally compelling is the passive drama of the hidden woman, which forms the psychological focus at the left (*Plate 11*). A tension is thus set up between the two protagonists in this scene, all the more powerful for being only suggested and not openly revealed.

The technical and compositional devices are, if not original with Sotatsu, certainly carried to a point of importance that had not hitherto been seen in Japanese art. Much has been written about Sotatsu's "invention" of the *tarashikomi* painting method, here seen in the detail of the pine tree (*Plate 16*), the roof of the cottage (*Plate 11*), and the rocks near the barrier gate (*Plate 12*). Actually this innovation of dropping one wet pigment over another to create a rich variation of tones is but a translation into color of a similar method seen in the overlapping ink blots of the "splash ink" method in black-and-white employed by Sesshu and the ink painters of Yüan China. Sotatsu here experiments with this technique but he does not relinquish the very effective flat areas of green that cut up the space with tremendous daring and incredible sureness. Silhouetted masses, rich color, and strong linear movements thus build up the stage set and emphasize the emotional forces that are enacted on this stage.

Sotatsu's striving for dynamic design culminates in the lively and continuous movement of these rushing divinities of the air. The Wind God (*Plates 18 & 20*) starts the motion by leaping down from the upper right and directs the eye leftward toward the Thunder God inside his circle of rattling drums (*Plates 17 & 19*). The floating draperies carry the motion back to its starting point, there to resume the course in an endless circulation of stormy air currents.

The suggested lines of motion have their concrete counterpart in the figures of the two divinities, each of which does not contain a single line that is not imbued with movement. But the different characteristics of these figures are incarnated in the curves of the "Wind," as contrasted with the jagged angles of the "Thunder"; by thus stressing the inner spiritual differences of these imaginary creatures, Sotatsu avoids the arbitrarily imposed, externally geometric motion that makes for monotony in much of High-Renaissance and Baroque art in Europe.

The achievement of this work earned Sotatsu the compliment of imitation by such eminent followers as Korin and Hoitsu, but faithful though their copies are they lack the inner vitality of the original creation.

The dynamic force that emanates from this design of two flying divinities may be attributed to the very nature of the theme, but it goes far beyond the requirements of the subject matter. The love of movement per se seems to have been a deep-rooted characteristic of Japanese art, which was often restrained by the influence of Chinese reasonableness and philosophic calm. Whenever Chinese domination subsided, Japanese art burst forth with examples of overt or hidden movement. The picture scrolls of the Kamakura period revel in scenes of rushing humanity excited by miracles, by

(continued on page 43)

Plate 19

←LIFT FOLD

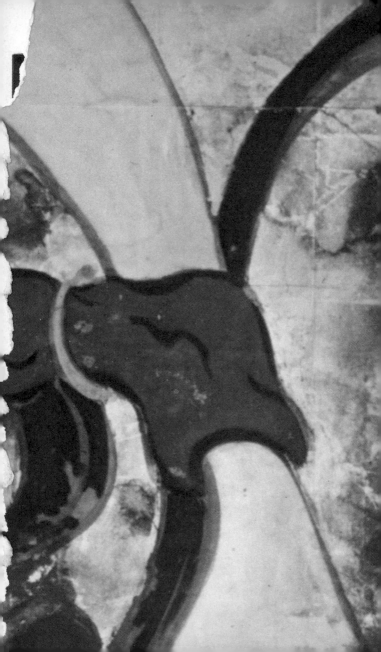

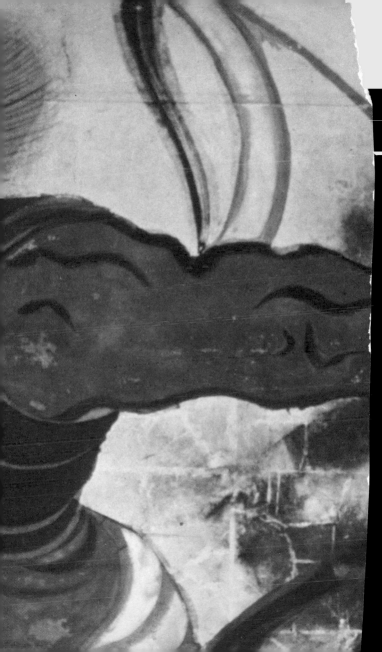

Plate 20

GODS OF THUNDER AND WIND

Pair of two-panel screens, gold foil and color on paper, 154×169 cm. each. Kenninji, Kyoto.

(continued from page 36)
hell-fire, or by the endless battles between the great clans. The sword thrust of Miyamoto Niten (1584–1645) penetrated into his ink painting. Even the renowned virtuosity of the Kano brush line, as practiced by Eitoku, Sanraku, or Tanyu, aimed at a simulation of speedy sureness. Through the great woodblock prints and down to our day, the most typical Japanese design prefers asymmetry, rhythmic unbalance, diagonal slashes, and uneasy inner tensions. Thus Sotatsu revealed a profound craving of the Japanese spirit when he turned back to themes that allowed an outlet for movement and speed.

Sotatsu's originality is all the more accentuated when the sources of this theme are analyzed Similar flying divinities occur in some pictorial scrolls of the Kamakura period; and a very close ancestry can be traced in two statues of the same gods of wind and thunder (attributed to Joben, Kamakura period) that stand in the Sanju-Sangendo Temple in Kyoto, where Sotatsu must surely have seen them. In the very act of taking on such traditional material and transforming it into a free creation, the full measure of Sotatsu's genius can be seen. He took the vocabulary of the theme and then created a new pictorial arrangement, filled with its own rhythmic and poetic compulsion.

This work also furnishes a summation of Sotatsu's technical procedure. In part he uses line or he omits it in the *mokkotsu* manner (i. e., "boneless," meaning without outlines); there are areas of flat pigment and other parts where the color is built up in several layers, with the thick white *gofun* painted over with wet drops of color melting into each other in the *tarashikomi* manner. And there are even traces of ink as a substructure of the design on the gold foil.

SCREENS WITH FAN PAINTINGS: FARMHOUSE IN EARLY SPRING; PUPPIES

From pair of two-panel screens decorated with fans, color on paper, each fan about 18.3×56.2 cm. Samboin Monastery, Kyoto. See also Plates 23 and 44–47.

This set of screens decorated with applied fan paintings provides a good example of the fusion of tradition and innovation, of conventionalization and fresh observation, that forms a basic trait in the work of Sotatsu. In this case he inherited a tradition of fan paintings that even in his day was hoary with age; and he lived in an epoch when the application of such fan papers to decorative screens was extremely fashionable. Numerous screens with fan designs have come down to our day and many of these are close to Sotatsu or to his school, leading even to the belief that he may have been the son of a fan merchant of Kyoto.

The two screens in the Samboin are relatively simple in arrangement, since they number only eleven fans placed on a neutral ground. The actual placement, however simple, is full of variety and subtle manipulation; such evidence of taste and fine proportion may be traced to Sotatsu himself, or it may have been left to the mounter, who, like many Japanese craftsmen, had a highly refined feeling for spatial arrangement.

To place the theme within the odd shape of each separate fan was a challenge to artistic ingenuity. Sotatsu sometimes followed the dictates of the curved fan shape and of the radiating ribs below, but more usually he composed freely, overriding the geometric restrictions of radius and circumference. The odd shape and the traditional form gave Sotatsu a welcome framework, which he accepted and within

(*continued on page 46*)

(*continued from page 44*)

which he moved with as much imagination as a great poet can move within the limits of the sonnet form.

Since the framework of grouped fans provided the skeleton of design that unified the whole screen, each single fan need not adhere to any narrative unity. The artist felt free to mingle historical and literary episodes with vignettes that are direct observation of details in nature, of flowers and playful animals, and of scenes from daily life. This free commingling of traditional and realistic episodes makes for a sparkling variety such as is also seen in the carvings of Gothic cathedrals.

For the artist's own development, these small scenes proved a testing ground for designs and techniques that were later used on a more monumental scale. The puppies, the oxen, the farm houses, and the flowering trees can readily be traced to the old pictorial scrolls that also furnished the literary subjects. Even on this small scale one can see them being "Sotatsu-ized" through his peculiar painting techniques and his special modes of simplification. One by one they later reappear, separate, enlarged, and treated with a broader vision, on the screens and in the ink paintings that form the more monumental part of Sotatsu's work.

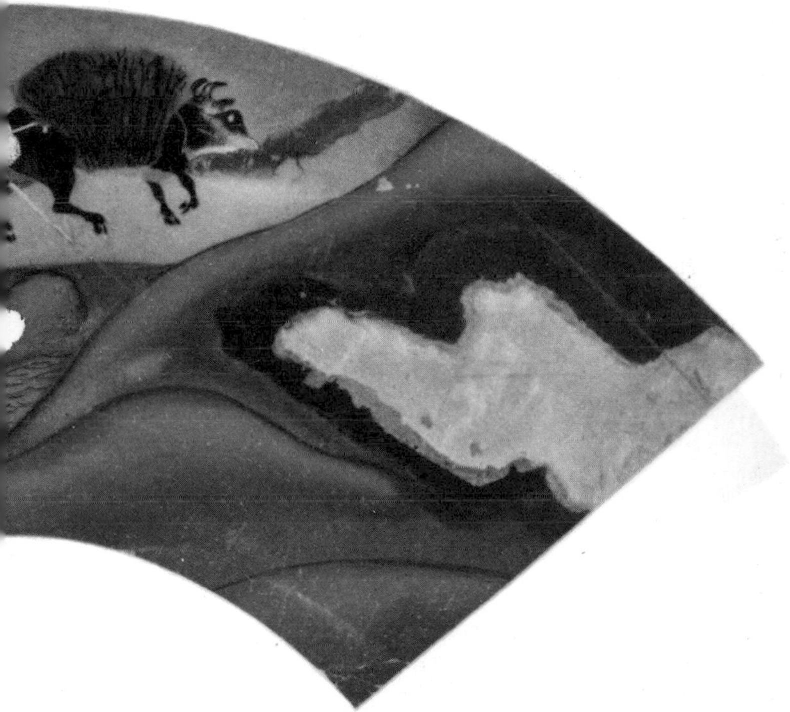

Plate 23. SCREENS WITH FAN PAINTINGS : COUNTRY SCENE WITH BULLOCK. *From same screens as Plates 21 & 22.*

Plate 24

"TALES OF ISE" ALBUM: WOMAN WRITING ON WATER

From an album illustrating "Tales of Ise," color on paper. Private collection.

There remain some forty small paintings by Sotatsu (or attributions of various degrees of authenticity) in the form of separate album leaves or *shikishi*. When such leaves are in sequence and when they deal with a single theme as do these illustrations from the *Tales of Ise*, it can be seen that this form derives from cutting the old pictorial scrolls into sections. Sotatsu's activity of copying such scrolls had familiarized him with the blending of writing and painting and he moved entirely at ease in this type of illustration.

As may be surmised, Sotatsu adheres closely to the literary subject and also to the old style of Yamato pictures in which these themes were painted from the eleventh century on. This archaic manner leads to the belief that these may be youthful works, in which the artist was trying his wings, produced before he took off on the more forceful and more original flights of his larger works.

The two pages shown here (*Plates 24 & 25*) both deal with
(*continued on page 50*)

Plate 25

"Tales of Ise" Album: Poem Written in Blood

From the same album as Plate 24.

(continued from page 48)
frustrated love. The woman who is trying to write upon the running brook illustrates a *waka* (31-syllable poem) which states that "It is more futile to yearn for a man who does not love me than to write on the surface of water." The second lady is even more tragic in her pain; running after her faithless lover, she has fallen exhausted to the ground. With her own blood she is now trying to write upon a rock her last sigh, which proclaims that she is exhausted unto death, since she could not retain her beloved.

The figures reveal at once their debt to the old pictorial scrolls of Ise and of Genji. The facial types, the long black hair, the rigid costume folds, all this is taken over without any attempt at transformation. A little more change creeps into the landscape details, which are somewhat "looser" in line and color than the ancient models of the Heian and Kamakura periods, but this obedient adherence to older forms is a long step behind the gradual liberation of the Genji screens or the "Ivy Walk."

Plate 26

FAN SCREENS: THUNDER GOD

Detail from pair of eight-panel screens decorated with fans, color on paper, 137 × 398 cm. each. Imperial Household Collection. See also Plates 27–31 and 34–35.

Screens decorated with applied fan paintings must have been very fashionable in the Kyoto of Sotatsu's day, to judge by the great number that have come down to us. Many of these were produced in a "workshop manner," some under the guidance of Sotatsu, and some having no connection with him other than that of time and place. Most closely connected with Sotatsu are the set in the Daigoji (*Plates 21–23 & 44–47*) and the pair of screens in the Imperial Household Collection (*Plates 26–31 & 34–35*).

This pair of screens is of huge dimensions and holds no less than forty-eight fans, which are scattered three to a panel with a fine sense of "thoughtful casualness."

There is no single theme to connect the fans; in fact, the greatest variety of subject seems to have been desired. A majority of the fans contains scenes of battle drawn from the Heiji-Hogen wars; these follow closely the ancient

(*continued on page 56*)

Plate 27

FAN SCREENS: PLUM BLOSSOMS

From same pair of screens as Plate 26.

(continued from page 55)
Kamakura period scrolls, sometimes to the point of identity.
Perhaps in order to avoid too noisy and martial a spirit,
there are interspersed fan designs of a poetic and atmospheric
nature.   From the *Tales of Ise* come such scenes as
" Akutagawa " (*Plate 26*), where the thunder god threatens
to prevent the abduction of a lady, or the domestic idyll
(*Plates 30-31 & 35*) with the lover observing through a
window how his mistress is filling a rice bowl.   The
former scene calls for a comparison with the Thunder God
screen (*Plate 19*), where the same theme was carried to far
greater heights of compositional refinement and dynamic
vitality.   Still more calm and relaxed are the fans with
pastoral scenes or the flowers and shrubs that are painted
with a wonderful blend of realistic observation and almost
abstract design.   In the " Woman Serving Rice " fan (*Plates*
(continued on page 58)

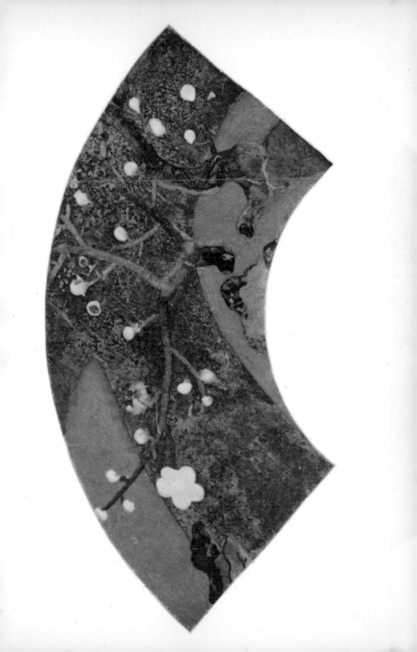

Plates 28 & 29 (following)

FAN SCREENS: DETAIL FROM "HEIJI-HOGEN WARS"

From same pair of screens as Plate 26.

(continued from page 56)
30-31 & 35), note how Sotatsu fits his story in the fan shape and lets the verticals of his design follow the radiating ribs of the fan—a rather rare instance of such "geometrization" in Sotatsu, who generally composes far more freely in this odd shape.

If we cannot state with assurance the degree of participation that involves Sotatsu with these screens, their overall taste is decidedly in his manner and their decorative effectiveness is indisputable. This type of work, plus the mention of a "Tawaraya" fan shop in Kyoto, has led to the supposition that Sotatsu may have emerged from such a fan-maker's establishment, that he soon distinguished himself above other craftsmen, and thus came to the attention of Koetsu and Mitsuhiro.

Plate 29

Plate 30 & 31. Fan Screens: Details from " Woman Serving Rice" (*see Plate* 35). *From same pair of screens as Plate* 26.

IVY WALK SCREENS : DETAILS

See Plates 8 & 9 for entire screens.

This set of screens is a relative newcomer to the circle of " works *by* Sotatsu " (rather than " attributed *to* Sotatsu "), and this identification is based strongly on the stylistic affinity it bears with several other works by the master. The combination of script and decoration allies it with several scrolls of decorated poems on which Sotatsu collaborated with Koetsu. Actually this pair of screens may be regarded as a monumental enlargement of such a scroll, with Sotatsu turning to the *Tales of Ise* for his subject of the narrow, ivy-covered lane. The writing in the upper part is by the hand of Karasumaru Mitsuhiro, the scholarly courtier who befriended Sotatsu.

The two screens are drawn into one compositional whole through a series of interlocking planes held in asymmetric balance. Green against gold is the color scheme, ascetically simplified, yet richly decorative and infinite in its space suggestion. Far more daring than in the Genji scenes is the departure from direct illustration and the transformation of the poem into a new form which is a visual equivalent created by the painter. Here is a culmination of a series of experiments in balancing writing and painting that may be analyzed as follows : The first steps are seen in the poetic scrolls done with Koetsu (*Plate 40*), in which the poetic content and the calligraphy definitely dominate, while the muted decoration forms a quiet counterpoint ; this is still a literary work to be held and read. The second stage occurs in the Genji screens (*Plates 6 & 7*), where the visual presentation and the narrative content are held in equal balance. The third step, seen in this Ivy screen, states with assurance that a screen is not a piece of literature, but a visual and tangible decorative element in a room, which may be enriched by the lyric mood of a poetic source. Such sensitive adjustments of literature and painting have no match anywhere in the world, and even in Japan this finesse was achieved only at this moment, in this rarefied aesthetic circle around the genius of Koetsu in Kyoto.

Plate 34

FAN SCREENS: DETAIL FROM " HEIJI-HOGEN WARS "

Fan painting from same pair of screens as Plate 26. See also Plates 28 & 29.

In a recent study Terukasu Akiyama (see Bibliography) has made a comparison between the original scroll of *Tales of Heike* and Sotatsu's versions of this theme. The resemblances are very close indeed, often to the point of identity. They leave no doubt about Sotatsu's familiarity with ancient Japanese scrolls, and with this Heike scroll in particular.

Fourteen fragments from the original scroll were collected in 1943. Several scenes recur in Sotatsu's fans and especially close are those dealing with the battle of Rokuwara. The rearing horses, the excited open mouths, even the man who is here seen " biting the dust," all are taken over with fidelity to the spirit of danger and excitement. Then the subject becomes " Sotatsu-ized," that is, adapted to his own decorative sense, fitted into the fan shape, and treated with the technical devices associated with this master.

Plate 35 (above). FAN SCREENS:
WOMAN SERVING RICE.
See Plates 30 & 31 for details.

Plates 36–38 (following). PAINTINGS ON CYPRESS DOORS. *Yogen-in Monastery, Kyoto.* Despite much repair and repainting, an emanation of Sotatsu's style can still be found here. The two fantastic lions show the influence of the great Kano Eitoku (legend has it that he was actually Sotatsu's teacher), who is credited with originating the Momoyama trend towards bold, decorative wall painting. Almost equally fantastic is the elephant painting attributed to Sotatsu. The imagination of Japanese artists was being aroused by hearsay reports of exotic animals across the seas, and in his characteristic fashion Sotatsu used such themes with naïve exuberance rather than any concern for realistic detail. The Yogen-in is located quite near the Sanju-Sangendo, thus affording Sotatsu ample opportunity to see the latter's Kamakura period statues of the Wind God and Thunder God, which were to stimulate his great screens on the subject.

Plate 36. ELEPHANT. *Painting on cypress door.*
See explanation opposite.

Plates 37 & 38. Lions. *Paintings on cypress*

doors. *See page 70 for explanation.*

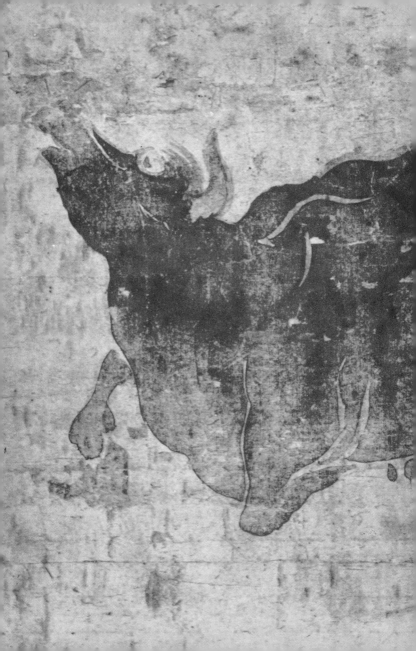

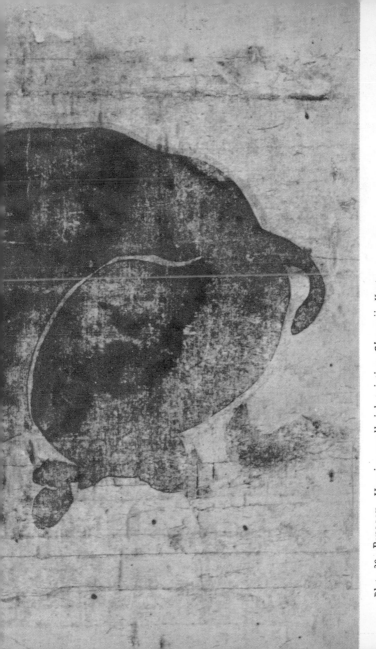

Plate 39. Bullock. *Hanging scroll, ink painting. Chomyoji, Kyoto.*

Plate 40. SECTION OF SCROLL OF POEMS. *Calligraphy by Koetsu and paintings by Sotatsu. Dan Collection.* Several scrolls in Japanese and American collections, with the unmistakable calligraphy of Koetsu, show a continuous type of decoration in washes of gold and silver paint. The example shown here is typical and also well substantiated in attributing the background paintings to Sotatsu. Without trying to "illustrate" the poems, the paintings carry on a sort of muted counterpoint to the music of the poems by creating a poetic mood. The poems are from the *Senzai Wakashu,* while Sotatsu's painting are a rendering of the four seasons. The decoration is believed to have been done first, in the characteristic pale washes of gold and silver that loom like dusky shadows beneath the vigorous accents of the calligraphy. The placement of writing against colored backgrounds decorated with "abstract" designs or scattered gold dust had been customary in Japan at least since the Heian period.

Plate 41.
PEONIES.
*Hanging
scroll, ink
painting.
Yasuda
Collection.*

(continued from page 22)

dancers are placed with the sole concern for the inner pictorial demands of the composition. By making use of the swirling tails, Sotatsu whips the movement from a slow start at lower right to a crescendo in which the dancers twist and leap. After the furious contraposto of the fourth dancer near the top (see *Plate 10* for detail), there is a pause and a change of tempo in the group at the left forming the involuted circle that rotates about its own axis. This separate group poses a problem of origin and style. There is a sort of Aztec ferocity and primitivism in the costumes and masks of these dancers, which the painter emphasized further

through his "fractional" rendering of the body, in which every figure is shown in a disjointed fashion, with feet and head in profile, while the shoulders are seen frontally. This device is familiar to us from Egyptian art, and it might pass unnoticed in this case as well if it were not so sharply contrasted with the skillfully rendered contraposto of the "king" in the other dance group. In other words, Sotatsu is for some reason deliberately mixing a primitive and a sophisticated approach to the representation of the human figure. The mystery behind this rendition makes that circular group appear strangely exotic and out of place in Sotatsu and in all of Japanese art.

Plates 44–47. FAN PAINTINGS.
From " Fan Screens " (see Plate 26).

Plate 48. PRIEST SAIGYO'S LIFE.
Section of a scroll. Mori Collection.

The most important document pertaining to the life and work of
Sotatsu is his copy of a picture scroll relating the life of Priest
Saigyo, "copied" from an ancient scroll; it bears as its colophon
an inscription by Karasumaru Mitsuhiro stating that the painting
was made by "Sotatsu Hokkyo" in the seventh year of Kanei (1630).
This brief mention forms the cornerstone of factual information

regarding the life and style of Sotatsu. What was expected from such a "copy" was not a slavishly exact reproduction, but a "new edition," as it were. Sotatsu does not hesitate to use his own style freely, even though he adheres quite closely to the content and to the archaic conventions of Yamato pictures.

INK PAINTINGS BY SOTATSU

With the newly developing fame of Sotatsu, an increasing number of ink paintings are coming to light and are attributed to this master with varying degrees of authenticity. Such small works are even more sparingly documented or recorded than the larger screens, and the criterion, in most cases, must rest on stylistic analysis alone.

The love of animals runs through all of the works connected with Sotatsu. He found these oxen, horses, and dogs frequently represented on the picture scrolls of the Kamakura period, where we can readily see them in the *Shigisan Engi*, the *Scroll of Fast Bullocks* (Seattle Museum), the *Adventures of Kibi in China* (Boston Museum), and many others. This tradition also stimulated direct observation of animals, which Sotatsu then carried over into his ink paintings and into the large screens. His approach is not scientifically anatomical, but proceeds directly to the essential character and movement of the animal. There is the very essence of gauche charm and naïveté in the questioning or exploring puppy (*Plate 2*). The cormorants pursue their life amidst the lotus flowers, which dominate them unrealistically in size, but are true to their real numerical dominance in the pond (*Plates 4 & 5*). The dashing and rearing horses on many fan paintings have a long and varied ancestry in Japanese and Chinese painting, reaching back at least one thousand years before Sotatsu.

The painter was especially fascinated by the tremendous strength within the fine specimens of bulls, which were trained to pull the heavy and ornate carriages of the daimyos on their travels. Sotatsu painted bullocks in all poses of strain and rest, until they became almost a signature of his work (*Plates 3 & 39*). Not since the prehistoric bison painted on the walls of Altamira had any artist brought such understanding to the vitality and sculptural bulk of these powerful creatures.

In these animal paintings in ink, Sotatsu developed certain stylistic and technical details that became his particular forte, if not his original creation. In the resting bull we can see clearly the procedure of painting directly in large areas of flowing ink, without any previous outline. This *mokkotsu*, or "boneless," technique forms a break with the virtuosity of the Chinese calligraphic brush strokes that were the special pride of the Kano artists.

Since Sotatsu avoided the sharp ink outlines, he had to resort to a method of separating anatomical masses in the bulls or the dog by means of "rivers" or borders left unpainted where areas meet but do not touch. This results in a simplification of shapes, resembling that of stencil printing, and imparts to Sotatsu's work an added quality of primitive simplicity and directness.

The peonies, lotus flowers, ivy leaves, and grasses that Sotatsu painted in a similar ink style, are also found in the gold and silver washes in the background of the poetic scrolls that bear Koetsu's fine calligraphy.

GLOSSARY

Ashikaga—family of shoguns who gave their name to the early part of the Muromachi perid, ca. 1331–1473

Bugaku—court dancing, with masks and musical accompaniment, originally imported from China in the Nara period, ca. 750

Edo—old name for Tokyo and also for the period when the government of the Tokugawa shoguns had its seat in that city, 1615–1868

Genji—name of one of the great feudal families, also known as Minamoto ; also refers to *The Tale of Genji*, famous novel written ca. 1020 by the court lady Murasaki Shikibu, recounting the loves of a handsome member of the family

Gofun —powdered clam shells, used as thick white underpainting on screens, etc.

Heian —old name for Kyoto and also for the period when that city was most important as the center of government and culture, ca. 781–1180

Heike (or Heiji) another great feudal family, also known as Taira ; archenemies of the Genji family

Ise Monogatari (*"Tales of Ise"*)—a tenth-century collection of poems and romances

Kamakura —a town near Tokyo ; seat of the shogunate government 1180–1331

Kano —a family of professional artists representing the Chinese tradition of ink painting in Japan ; flourished ca. 1500–1700

Momoyama (*"Peach Hill"*)—site of a castle outside Kyoto and name of the period 1575–1615

Muromachi —a section of Kyoto containing the homes of the Ashikaga shoguns ; name of the period 1392–1568

Mokkotsu (*"boneless,"* i. e., *without lines*)—technique of painting in washes of ink or water color, without linear drawing

Shogun—title of military governors or dictators

Suiboku (*"water ink"*)—painting with light and dark washes of *sumi*

Sumi —black ink derived from pine charcoal ; also known as Chinese ink or "India ink"

Tarashikomi —technique of dropping water color on still-wet underpainting

Tea ceremony —a social ritual externalizing some Zen principles of thinking, behavior, and aesthetics

Tokugawa —name of the family of shoguns who ruled 1615–1867 ; also alternate name for the Edo period

Tosa —a family of painters and name of their school and style ; flourished ca. 1300–1500

Yamato —name for the "heartland" of Japan, the region around Nara ; also name of painting style ca. 900–1300 and later revived

Zen—a branch of Buddhism stressing meditative practice leading to direct enlightenment

SELECTED BIBLIOGRAPHY

Works in Western Languages Mentioning Sotatsu

Fenollosa, Ernest F. *Epochs of Chinese and Japanese Art.* New York and London, 1912, 1921, Vol. 2, pp. 129–36, passim. (Note confusions between Sotatsu and others of this school.)

Moriya, Kenji. *Die Japanische Malerei.* Wiesbaden (Brockhaus), 1953, pp. 100–03.

Munsterberg, Hugo. *The Landscape Painting of China and Japan.* Tokyo (Tuttle), 1955, pp. 113–14.

Pageant of Japanese Art, edited by staff members of National Museum. Tokyo (Toto Bunka), 1953, Vol. 2. pp. 30–31, 75–78.

Paine, Robert T. *Ten Japanese Paintings in the Museum of Fine Arts, Boston.* 1939.

——, and Soper, Alexander. *The Art and Architecture of Japan.* Harmondsworth (Pelican), 1955, pp. 112–16.

Warner, Langdon. *The Enduring Art of Japan.* Cambridge (Harvard), 1952, pp. 67–69.

Works in Japanese on Sotatsu

Akiyama, Terukasu. "Heiji Monogatari," in *Yamato Bunka,* VII, July, 1952.

Fukui, Rikichiro. "Decorative Art of the Momoyama and Tokugawa Periods," reprint of a lecture, in *Bijutsu,* 1926.

Nakagawa Chujun. *Tawaraya Sotatsu.*

Sotatsu Gashu (Collected Works of Sotatsu), Tokyo (Shimbi Shoin), 1913.

Sotatsu-Korin Ha Zuroku (Illustrated Catalogue of Exhibition of the Sotatsu-Korin School at the National Museum, Tokyo, 1951), Kyoto (Benrido), 1952.

Tanaka, Ichimatsu. *Sotatsu.* Tokyo (Kodansha), 1955.

Tanaka, Kisaku. "Sotatsu Zakko" and "Sotatsu Zakko Zoku" (Miscellaneous Sotatsu Studies), in *Bijitsu Kenkyu,* Nos. 20, 23, September, November, 1930.

Tani, Shin-ichi. "A Study of Sotatsu," in *Kokka,* Nos. 478, 480, September and November, 1930.

——. *Sotatsu.* Toyo Bijutsu Bunko.

Tokugawa, Yoshitaka. "Sotatsu's Ink Painting," in *Zauho,* No. 1.

Yashiro, Yukio. "Essay on Sotatsu (regarding works in American collections)," in *Yamato Bunko,* 10–12.

——. "The Matsushima Screen in the Freer Collection, Washington," in *Bijutsu Kenkyu,* 1938.

——. "Ise Monogatari Album," in *Bijutsu Kenkyu,* No. 98, February 1940.